The Evolution of Her Perception

The Evolution of Her Perception Copyright © 2024 by Trenessa McNulty

All rights reserved.

For privacy reasons, some names, locations, and dates may have been changed.

Warning: This book contains sensitive subject matter, including discussions of self-harm, suicide, explicit sexual content, and rape. Reader discretion is advised.

Book Cover by Trenessa McNulty
Illustrations by Trenessa McNulty
2024

ISBN: 979-8-218-42516-6

Dedication

This piece of art was written for all of the tender-hearted lovers who do not receive the same love they emit to the world. I see you. I understand you. I am you. You are loved, you are cherished, and you are worthy.

Trenessa McNulty, Author

Let all that you do be done in love.

1 Corinthians 16:14

Grandma Becky, your love has enveloped me during this writing process. Thank you for watching over me and showing up in ways I never experienced while you were here. I love and cherish you now and forever more.

Rest in Peace

Rebecca Louise Williams

The Evolution of Her Perception

Preface

This book took ten years to complete. Ten years of many lonely nights and getting lost in the rooms of my mind. Ten years of asking myself, "Why?" Ten years of being burdened by cognitive dissonance. It started as a mission to become a better version of myself for other people. I wanted to be a better daughter, lover, sister, and friend. It began when I was a child, as most of our traumas and learned behaviors do. I don't remember the nights I spent with my mom in a homeless shelter. I don't have memories of my grandparents gaining custody of me, or however the story goes, though I will say the best memories I do have, were with them. I don't remember some of these defining moments, but my body does. My DNA, made up of generational trauma that didn't even belong to me, was forced to reprogram once I became aware of toxic, repeated patterns. I've learned, I've unlearned, and I've relearned–and I decided to be the healer of my bloodline.

Most of my memories from childhood, I've tried deadening them. I'd be lying if I said that good times didn't exist. When I was younger, my mother and I had such a strong bond. We would get my little sister and brother to bed, I'd go to her room and, we would watch TV together. One of my favorite memories was when we watched an episode of Saturday Night Live. Will Ferrell, being the absolute idiot that he is, had our stomachs aching from laughing at his character in the skit "More Cowbell". That was just one memory I hadn't let go of, and maybe it seems so tiny to those reading these words, but it was one of the few times I had my mom to myself–our quality time. Reflecting on this memory created a full-circle moment for me that I will explain a bit later.

I remember being by my mama's side wiping tears off her face. These tears, of course, stemmed from my stepfather being in the streets. I'm sure being a young mother brought on much of her stress and sadness, wanting a better life for herself. But he was definitely the bulk of her problems–emotionally, at least. I remember the big arguments they would get into, especially my mother, begging him not to leave. She would fall apart, clinging to his legs as he tried to leave the house. I was there when my stepfather wasn't. He spent years in and out of jail and prison. As I got older, the relationship between my mother and me became nonexistent. Maybe he kept going to jail as a vacation; after all, when she was miserable, we all were. Her misery, again, was birthed by lies and broken promises of fidelity topped with the cherry of her own self-limiting beliefs.

I blamed my stepfather for my lack of happiness, and over the years, he never once sat me down and asked how his absence affected me. Of course, it hurts to see his own blood disappointed in his behavior and abandonment, but were my feelings ever considered? Did they not matter because I was another man's child? He never asked me how absolutely broken it made me to have a second chance at a father and he failed as well.

The passion I had to help my mom diminished over time, as she was no longer feeding me words of affirmation. She used to notice the little things I did to help her and show my love. It turned into unappreciated expectations. When those words from my mom halted, so did my confidence. I felt like I wasn't valued. Truth is, at least my truth from the perspective of my adolescent mind at the time; she didn't seem to care about anything unless my stepfather was in the room.

I remember babysitting, making dinner, and getting my siblings to bed. I even knew when my mom would be home from work, so I'd run her bathwater on time to make sure it was still hot once she made it home. Afterward, I'd rub her feet and talk her to sleep, telling her about my day or asking questions that required a quick Google search. I was 8 years old. I grew up fast, and as much as I loved my mother, I resented her. Why did I resent her? Was it because my childhood was filled with adult responsibilities? Or maybe because my stepfather was deemed her favorite, and all he contributed was pillow talk and financial relief? I played the role of the husband because I hated seeing my mom upset and struggling all the time. Maybe it was my stepfather's lack of effort that encouraged my will to people-please and go above and beyond. I mean, I was always doing something to gain my mother's approval and keep a smile on her face. I thought my acts of service were enough to bring her happiness.

My mother fought for the love and attention of my stepfather, while I worked for hers. It wasn't only her love. I think I tried gaining my stepfathers, too. I'd cook them anniversary meals, put on Sade, and set up cute little living room picnics with candlelight's. Making sure to focus on all the details. I'd get my siblings together to put on talent shows for their entertainment and make hand-made cards for them. I was always so proud in the moments I was serving, but I think it was the recognition I loved just as much as their reactions. It was the praise. Not to say that I did any of it with the expectation to receive that praise and recognition, but therapy and self-reflection over the years have revealed to me my need for validation and my need to be needed–to be seen.

Now, here's the full circle moment. During the stages of healing my mother-wound, it dawned on me that all my siblings, during their younger years, got all of my mother. Her attention, her love, her affection. Whereas I only had her in increments. They received her nurturing and her fight. I was overshadowed by a broken heart, poor decisions with lovers, and teenage priorities. By the time my mom got me back, she had my brother. Not too long after that, my little sister and it became one after another. I missed the most essential bonding years with my mom; I didn't get the best version of her. This realization inundated me with the pervasive belief I've held onto–that I've never been seen as deserving of being prioritized, consistently placed last, and regarded solely as an option because of my reliability. I was "a sorry excuse of a daughter" to my parents, "a sorry excuse of a sister" to my brother, and "a sorry excuse of a woman" to my first partner. How could I not believe I was anything more than a "sorry excuse"? A disappointment? I needed to prove my worth. Prove why I'm a good friend to keep around, or a good daughter, or partner. Those same increments I got from my mom spilled over into my relationships. I got their praise and adoration sparingly, without much intention, just the stroking of their egos..and other things. A constant need for validation is an illness and one that almost killed me.

Though a triggering statement, when negative thoughts flood our minds, some call it the "lies of the enemy", but that is why perception is so important. Satan is often the scapegoat when it comes to our sins and decisions, but what people really lack is accountability—not godliness. In a way, over these past ten years, I was healing the perception I had of my mother while healing myself. Outside of her title, she's still like anyone else. Having her own guilts, fears, disappointments, feelings, traumas, failures, and unmet dreams.

I haven't been fair in placing all the fault on my mom, it's just that I barely know my dad enough to really have an opinion other than "absent". I'll never forget my dad taking me to the mall and buying me an outfit and a clean pair of white Air Force 1s for my birthday. It was a green striped shirt, some light wash jeans with diamond accents, and a neon green belt. I wore that outfit for three days. I was so proud of my daddy, and the time I got to spend with him. I kept him on a pedestal, thinking that he wanted a relationship, and it was my mom that kept me away. There is some truth in that, as he wasn't living his best life, but neither was my stepdad and she always made him the exception. Even so, the effort just wasn't there. It was always me reaching out to him. Even when it came to that side of my family. I just never felt like I fit in. No one ever called to check on me or wanted to make plans. Anytime I saw anyone, it was because I visited. I showed up to events, parties, cookouts, birthdays, and holidays—when invited. But very rarely did my family show up for me.

Once my grandmother died, it sent me into a spiral. To this day, 3AM calls always stir a panic. I didn't just lose her, but all the stories and knowledge she had of our family history. I lost moments of cooking her meals and hearing her rave about how good my recipes are. I lost getting to know her at her core. I knew everything about my mother's side but nothing about my fathers. Her passing is what encouraged my dabble in spirituality. I needed to feel her presence again. I needed her to speak through the heavens and guide me. And she did.

It took me a long time to step outside of myself and try to understand those who hurt me. My mother, 19, and the daughter of parents who didn't believe in mixing races. They weren't even at the hospital when I was born. I can't imagine how she felt experiencing childbirth for the first time without her mom holding her hand and comforting each push to bring me into this world. Her heart was torn from disappointment and knowing that my dad wouldn't be a present father and partner. She was shattered and alone. The same love and attention I sought from her is the same love and attention she needed from her parents. Their nurturing, their support. I think she would've even accepted a slap across the face that day. Anything to feel like she was at least worth the visit. That's only my guess. Are you starting to see the cycle?

The false belief of not being good enough followed me into adulthood. At twenty-two, I thought I was finally worth the keeping. I was engaged to who I thought would be my forever. He had us all fooled, at least in the beginning. He noticed things about me that no one else had before. Like how my lips are perfectly outlined (he even used the same reference my mom used to make about them looking like a little turtle's mouth). You would've thought I was God the way he worshiped me. I later learned the term I was experiencing was "love bombing" and that he did. He wrote me poems and even published a book titled, "Poems About Her". He made me feel like the only woman in the world. He made my birthdays special again after proposing on my twenty-third birthday. He was a people person, a charmer. It took two short months to destroy what we had been building for over a year. Sure, it was a short relationship, but I hoped to share the same story as my grandparents. They met and were married in a matter of months and have been married for 50+ years now. We opened a shared bank account he later used to steal 19 thousand dollars from before moving across the country. His lies started to catch up with him– and I, being the gullible lover I was, believed every single one of them because what is love without trust? He moved to Wyoming, which was another lie I learned. He was actually in Salt Lake City, Utah. I was picking out our wedding venue with his mother while he was caring for another woman and her baby. Which later turned into two women and two babies and in less than a month, eight women had reached out with screenshots of their relationships with him. He was a con artist.

I didn't want to believe them. I felt embarrassed at how much I begged him to unblock me. I even texted the other women to tell him how badly I wanted to fix us. But once his lies were revealed, he disappeared. "I promised you the world, Trenessa Johnson, and that's what I'll do!" One of many sweet messages he'd send that later turned into him telling me to kill myself (which I had a few attempts), all because his deceit had exposed him. I had to heal myself. I had to once again heal from damage that I didn't create. After the end of that relationship, I chose to remain abstinent for three years. During this time, I struggled with deep-seated feelings of inadequacy and mistrust towards men. I found myself grappling once again with those self-limiting beliefs: Why wasn't I good enough?

Romantic relationships often serve as mirrors, reflecting back the unhealed wounds of our inner child. In my case, these relationships brought to light my anxious-avoidant attachment style, characterized by a constant push and pull. I found myself repeatedly attracting partners who exhibited avoidant behaviors, retreating when things became too uncomfortable, or seeking validation elsewhere. This pattern took a toll on my self-esteem and left me questioning my worth.

I lived my life with a victim state of mind, believing that bad things happen to me rather than understanding that all things happen for me. I choose how to view a situation. I wasn't holding myself accountable for ignoring the red flags or not standing firm on the boundaries I enforced. Yes, a lot of these beliefs and thoughts were fed to me through other people's experiences and projections, but it was also my fault for not standing in my truth and knowing who I am. It was my fault; all the time I wasted being sad and depressed over feelings that move on like clouds. It was my fault for not taking the time to love myself. It was my fault for craving love so badly that I didn't assess people. It was my fault for trusting so easily. So fucking easily that it got me raped (I do not take responsibility for the act itself. Fuck that nigga). I, unfortunately, see the good in everyone and their demons.

O, the novel I'd write if I took every detail of my life and placed it on these pages. All the pain and sadness. All the lessons. All the disappointments. All the abuse. Instead, I wanted to pinpoint the roots from which I've had to learn to release myself. It's important to note that a lot of these big feelings were created in my mind as an adolescent. It was how I processed, as I didn't know how to at the time. My mother loved the best way she knew how, and just like myself, she has evolved and grown over the years.

Healing looks a lot like an iceberg. We see the tip and think, "Okay, I think I can handle this." but it's what we cannot see that torments us the most. The Titanic is a perfect visual example. The ship's captain saw the iceberg on the surface and it appeared much smaller than it actually was. He only considered its impact once it was too late. I wanted to highlight an important concept when it comes to healing and how trauma will continue to poison the bloodline until it's recognized and worked through. Most of the pain I experienced was from the projection of others. Their own hidden icebergs, their own disappointment in themselves, their own traumas and self-limiting beliefs, and their own lack of self-awareness and accountability. Like anyone, I adopted those beliefs, and they became my identity. I became a product of my environment, and my environment was sick. The truth is, yes—I am an emotional being. But that is my power. It takes a powerful, resilient, humble soul to still believe in the many shades of love when all I've ever felt is rejection and deep-seated self-hate for not ever feeling enough. It was never anyone's job to understand my feelings but my own. Few can empathize, and maybe that's what I've been wanting all these years. Someone to sit me down and say, "I see you. I understand you." but the only validation I ever needed was my own. And that is where true healing begins. Accountability. Recognizing my faults and triggers. Unlearning those behaviors and setting myself free from tormenting thoughts and beliefs. Becoming less reactive. Removing my ego and the poison from my tongue so I could stop repeating and inflicting trauma. That is what heals the bloodline. Healthy change. Enforcing boundaries. Creating safe spaces.

I needed you, my reader, to fully capture who I am at my core. I love through understanding, hoping to be a light to those who have ever felt like me. My gift to the world is a more healed version of myself, but my purpose is to be the example. I've shared my kindness and nurturing with the world because it's what *I* needed. And so, before dissecting the pieces of my soul shared in these poems, I will leave you with lyrics from Sade Adu that have always brought me back to myself. May these words paint the picture of Trenessa; the lover, the healer, and the little girl inside the woman. This is the story. The poems are the experience. Let's take a journey.

17

"Girl you are rich, even with nothing. And you know tenderness comes from pain. It's amazing how you love. Love is kind and love can give and get no gain. It's down the rugged road you've come. Though you had every reason, you didn't come undone. Somehow you made it to the other side. You didn't suffer in vain. You forgive those who trespass against you, and you know tenderness comes from pain. It's amazing how you love; and love is kind, and love can give, and love needs no gain."

-Sade Adu

The Evolution of Her Perception

/fēlz/

There is a certain divinity in making people feel
And that is what I do
I allow you to see parts of yourself that no one
knew were there except for you
That's how attentive I am
I listen to all your thoughts that form into words
and never once feel unsafe by the maniacal
ideas that have waltzed so beautifully
from your mind to your lips
I make you feel
I make you think about everything you've kept so hidden
Beautiful eyes don't always reflect the ocean
Yours are fierce, yet sad
Experienced, yet lost
They're paused--scared almost
Like staring back into mine
causes a nervous so vulnerable
and that's why I get pushed away
I've intricately described every part of you
No one likes to feel
Everyone wants to be noticed but never studied beyond the surface
Soon enough you'll learn–I make you feel
So that you'll heal

Parallels

My greatest heartbreak wasn't from a lover
It was my stepdad and solidified by my mother

"A sorry excuse for a daughter"
Those words pierced me at seventeen
And everything went dull
except for the blade against my skin

That blade made me feel when those words left me numb
I was too scared of death, so the grave I couldn't succumb
At least if I bleed I know I'm alive
Even feeling morbid inside

My sleeves grew longer trying to hide my creativity
Even when the hot summer came, they never noticed me

Some months had passed and school was my relief
Homecoming queen, I thought I'd finally been seen
But it was a class joke filled with cruelty
And once again, I started to bleed

Where does one find safety from the bullies in school halls
when they live on the other side of your bedroom walls?

To The Three Youngest

I wish I had more memories of us
But pain kept me away
I hit behind resentment
Forced maturity made me this way

I used to climb in trees
and have adventures in the woods
I used to make y'all laugh and smile
When no one else could

I used to race on bikes
And play with Barbie dolls
I used to put on fashion shows
In dirty overalls

I know I hurt y'all deeply
Running from my trauma
I had so much I needed to heal
From insecurities and mama

I miss the sister I used to be
Before mental health took a toll
I pray that y'all forgive me
Because I was a broken soul

I wish I had cuddled you more
And wiped away your tears
I wish I spent more time
Learning all your fears

I know that we're much older now
And time we can't get back
But hopefully you know I love you
To the moon and that's a fact

Cancer

Can I share with you a lie
That we both believed were true?
We bonded over pain for years
Believing our last names weren't as valued

The two McNulty's, we were quite the pair
You were my first best friend
And any time we fussed and fought
It was us until the end

Remember our adventures
Finding treasures in the woods?
We weren't taking no hikes
Without a backpack full of food

I chased you with kitchen knives
And you choked me til I saw black
But we always stuck together
Always had each others back

Although we share the same last name
And we felt we didn't belong
The truth is that we are beyond loved
The lies, they were so wrong

Banana

Before jealousy became my new name
You were my baby doll
I loved holding you and being a big sister again
I was excited finding out you were a girl

I can't put a finger on when the lies began
My perception tainted as a child
But I remember the love in mama's eyes
It was enough to drive me wild

I knew I'd been replaced
And I hated you for years
You experienced daddy daughter moments
And all mine did was bring on tears

The relationship you have with mama
Yeah, that should've been me
I know we had fun times growing up
But those memories, they flee

You were the ideal daughter
The perfect girl next door
Popular amongst your friends
And chosen to play sports

You always kept a stable job
And made mama so proud
I hated you so much because
She loved you out loud

I know my thoughts can be misconstrued
Full of little lies
But there were so many moments
You were seen as the prize

I love you little sister
Although it may not seem
I have to heal this wound of mine
Because around you, I don't feel seen

Inner Child

I am one with the ocean
Enraged, my waves reach new heights
In stillness, I reflect the light
Being reactive comforts my ego
While my soul fights for calm
I am one with the ocean
Inner child so soft
and emotions strong

Oldest Daughters

I think it started with you–I watched you chase
Disturbing even as a child
but I was too young to put it into words

The way you begged and fell to the ground
pleading for him to stay–quite sickening
If only you fought this hard to keep our relationship
maybe you'd accept our mirrors

You grew me in your womb and once our eyes met
you swear that was the moment you knew love
But you took it from me and gave it to men
who did not value my first home–you

I've always wanted love, but not the kind you received
You were used to tainted love
Your self-esteem bidding on the hearts of men
foreign to commitment and a mockery of your value

You wanted to be chosen by your partners
And I wanted to be chosen by you
You set the tone and I followed suit
Taking pages from your book–now mirrors once again

Rejected Melanin

I figured out who I am and now they hate me
My environment not so much a reflection of all my roots
I guess you could call me whitewashed
Yet, my father, the blackest man I know
And I only found significance in skin whiter than snow

I used to want my children white
A repulsing projection I had
And when I thought of bearing child
Embarrassing was my math

My mom is white, which makes me half white
My husband would be full
And half plus a whole equal...emptiness

Sickening to know those thoughts were alive
To be so angry with my father I'd degrade my own kind
The ignorance. The self-hate. No knowledge of my roots
Twas the start of evolution so I laced up my boots

They're mad I nestled in my truth, internalized racism extinct
Now I love every ounce of me, a black woman indeed
My skin bears magic and my curls pirouette with pride
They only hate me now because I've exposed my dark side

Baxley

I didn't give you permission to pierce my soul the way you did
But out of my love for you, I endured
You were cunning, attracted to my naivety and need for validation
You saw me as your prey and I only ever saw you
as the love of my life
How does it feel to deceive?
What chapter in the Book of Manhood
did you take those notes from?
Your cruelty was learned and you were at the top of your class
The Grand Master of Lies–and I believed every single one
Thousands of miles away
I loved you. I supported you. I took care of you
I ***trusted*** you
You painted our future in watercolors using my tears
You promised me a lifetime
Who would've thought that
the same lips that formed to say I love you
told me to stop the heart that beat solely for you?
5 years I've prayed to God, "Please piece me back together"
This journey has been long and grueling
with many lessons along the way
And if there's anything I have left to say
It is this—thank you

To Cure A Clouted Heart

How peculiar it is to give love
 and not be accepting of it.
The secret? It is simple.
You cannot give a love
that you reject.

So how do you accept it?

Start with yourself, my dear.
You deserve the world.
The world does not deserve you.

Muse

I decided to stop searching for a muse
It led me down roads paved in hurt
I could never spell "muse"
without "U"
So, that was my mission
To love you
Every ounce of you
From the richness of your skin
to the plummets of your soul
It killed me knowing that
I was always good
But not good.. enough
I was always beautiful to you
But not beautiful.. enough
A year later and I'm still on this
bullshit journey
But what I've learned
in the beauty of it all is this
I can't spell muse without
"Me"

Anthophile

I learned to appreciate flowers
observing them up close or afar
but never being selfish enough to
stunt their growth
I learned how to appreciate them
without the physical touch

I find beauty in the pigment of the petals
I find beauty in the crispness of the stem
I find beauty in the scent it shares with me

That's what love is
Lacking possession and selfishness
Observing without judgment
Free-flowing yet powerful
A spiritual experience

That is love.

Within Reach

Deep thoughts while staring at the ocean
The waves rolling over each other in gentle folds
My skin, sticky and tasting of the purest salt
Sand finding an attractiveness to my most intimate crevices
And my hair in its free-est, spiraled form
I don't quite know where I'm going, but it's within reach
Unlike my view of the ocean's horizon
That horizon holds secrets far better than the darkest side of the moon
It holds my dreams just over the plunge
Daring me to trust it's void
I see my dreams slip away
every time I give my power to fear
The wave of excuses forms and builds into a deadly force of nature
And just before I give up completely
I'm hit with the Tsunami of life
Pulling all of my ideas so far away from shore
then forcing them into action back towards me
Nature and stillness have a way of recreating your reality
And all the dreams I've dreamed of coming true
have now all come within reach

//<Self.Less>//

When I feel like dirt
I remember that the most beautiful things
are nurtured by it
and nurtured by me
So I'll be the dirt as you're the flower
I'll continue to stay hidden and kept away
I'll soak up just enough rain to quench my thirst
Then allow you to grow from the rest
The sun is yours

Sweetest of Skin

He made the nectar of Agave jealous–Sweetness was he
Each touch creating a wet mess in me
The way his mouth formed when the words "I love you"
flowed so eloquently from his lips,
made every promise I ever heard before irrelevant

No matter how beautiful they sounded
they were never enough to keep me because actions never followed
They say love is a verb
and his entangled me in ways unceasing

His words weren't just kisses to my ears
but they flicked the very flower I'd kept hidden
buried in all my roots–not willing to let any tree
muster up enough confidence to poke me with his branches

Shoulder kisses felt like butterflies
dancing after their metamorphosis
I thank God for him every day
For he is the sweetest of skin

The Other Golden Rule

Commitment would rather be friends
with consistency, than intent

NAAAA.

37

I've evolved past forgiveness laced in blunts and hidden in elevated laughter. The words, "I'm sorry", never left the lips of those I journeyed different consciousness with. Only a firm handshake with Mary Jane and the sweeping of my pain under Persian rugs–and my, how dusty they've become.

Anointed

I wasn't the first choice for men to fall at my feet
Not because I wasn't beautiful–because I hold a certain energy
They know that I am too good for them.
At least that's what mama said

"Trenessa, they see God in you, and turn the other way"
But my insecurities cried out
"You're my mom. That's what you're supposed to say"

I started observing the morals of my friends
and studying their insecurities
Their sex appeal was the main attraction–something I lacked
I didn't know how to use a body I hated
to attract a man who would love it; a man who would love me

Peer pressure slapped me clean across the face
and I soon became a reflection of the friends I hung around
Accepting of whatever attention I could get
and still, those men never wanted to lay me down

I guess my mom was right
because the excuse was always
"You're a good girl, you ain't ready"
Maybe it wasn't the love of God that they saw
It had to have been the fear
Either way, I am divinely guided and protected

When She Blooms

Like a lotus, she is buried in the mud
Absorbing all that the earth has for her
and accepting her flaws and imperfections
before opening her petals to the world

She is mysterious. She hides herself. She loves but it's sheltered
Keeping herself enclosed is how she heals and protects herself
You can look but only when she's ready
You can touch but only if you are the sun
For she only blooms for a light that warms her ever-flourishing soul

She only emerges from the depths of darkness
for a love so on fire that hell is envious
She will be hard to love at first
Because the world only notices that she comes from mud
And very few have stayed patient enough to see her unfold
into an array of vivid petals on the smooth tops of the water

She will capture your heart before you ever capture hers
But that's what it's like for a lotus
She will be kept hidden from the world
waiting for her sun to shine his light in her
for her beauty to unravel and be admired

But when she blooms...
He must be ready to stay her sun forever

Pure Intent

Will you let me live in your skin?
I wanna learn everything about you
so I can love you the right way
and be your safe space

Those other lovers didn't indulge
in the details of you
the way I do

Parabolas

Our curves tell a story
Your hands grip perfectly into the dips of mine
while my mouth waters around yours
The perfect equation

Suppressed

You expose me way too often
but not in the ways that are healthy
Sure—eventually you share me
with those you value most
but do they hold the capacity
to understand me the way you do?

You need rest.

Lighting a blunt immediately
upon your return home
Who knew you could get so high
while your heart plunges to its depths?

Why are you trying to hide me now?
I want to heal you—but you have to accept me.

Love always,
Feelings

Soul(ar) Eclipse

How jealous is the moon
When I gaze into the soul of the sun?
One hugging me with warmth
The other forcing me to face my inner being
And both fighting for the attention of me

Do they not know I am the iris of the sky
when both aligned?

Midnight Shots

Palo Santo fills the room
Eliminating energies
I meditate. To God I pray
Then drink the spirits willingly

This is healing for now.

Temporary Bliss

I went to the mountains today
and I felt like the tiniest speck on earth
seeing all of God's creations welcoming me
as if I'm the chosen one to love and nurture them

The trees made soft sounds
as the wind blew so peacefully
Leaves singing in my ears
The sun tickled my shoulders with kisses
while bumblebees danced in my curls

Gratitude showered over me
then a piercing in my heart
Remembering my time with you
May I not fall apart

Only for a moment, my mind was at ease

Bitter Nectar

What was it that intrigued you?
Why me? Why this broken vessel?
Is it because you know that once you're finished
 plucking my wet honeysuckle, you'll suddenly disappear
with no desire to woo me further
because you got the single drop that made me whole?

After suckling the roundness of my breasts
And feeding off of my inner thighs
You roll over and close your eyes
No intimacy. No holding me. No sweet whispers in my ear

I opened every part of me because I loved every ounce of you
I would've nurtured our children, instead, I swallowed
Your lips refusing the taste of mine
Your reassurance was an illusion, a beautiful lie you'd tell
My intuitive radar read the meter of your words all too well

How can you be a real nigga, scared of the truth?

Kalopsia

The smell of you is intoxicating. The sight of you is breathtaking.
And my future with you is what I was navigating
Trying to make you into the man that your father could never be
Trying to forever love you knowing your heart didn't lead

Instead of investing every ounce of you into a very small me
Not small in a physical sense but small, like self-love will never
intercede
And that's what led you to me
That's why the birds never met the bees
my womb could never hold half of you
Because you'd never hold all of me

And I loved you

I remember laying in your arms as you stroked my hair with your
fingers
Soaking up each second I had with you
I painted candy-coated pictures of a life that was ours
But you were a Sour Patch kid, sweet then sour
And inconsistencies began stacking like towers

I thought that the broken pieces of me
And the shattered pieces of you
would create a mosaic so beautiful and true
But instead, it was chaos misconstrued
And the thought of ever being art with you
Disappeared

Every word that danced from your lips

tickled every part of my body
Then those words came back to haunt me
Because intentions are actions that haven't yet happened

Your intentions became lies
So forgive me if I don't get excited anymore
I could never get attached to the thrill of broken promises
Maybe that's why I never married your excuses
I'm better than that

I wanted you. I craved you. I longed for you
You wanted my body. You loved my mind
But you weren't in tune with your own
You did nothing for me
Only tasting the honey between my thighs
Oh, but baby...
I broke my heart for you

Starving

I never delighted in the taste of breadcrumbs until you came along
I keep falling for your I miss you's, knowing you only want
 to see if I'll ignore my boundaries for you
So when you boldly asked, I foolishly gave in once more

And so repeats the cycle–until you miss me again.

Wet imaginations

It wasn't the way your lips formed around my clit
But the way you held your tongue there
Like you were learning the circumference of my imagination

I never knew what drowning was until you tipped my head back
And dispersed all your happiness in one swift motion
Down the back of my throat, your seeds sought a womb to plant into
You grab me by the hair as I submit myself to our favorite position

You pinned me down, spread me open, and went for a swim
Plunging into the wetness of my shallows
The most euphoric of places
And because you're claustrophobic
You don't like tight spaces
But this was your favorite one

We had fun
In our wet imaginations

Repeat

The emotions come and go like waves
Some are subtle and unharming while others crash and destroy
I won't go too far into specifics but tonight they crashed
They dismantled any and every positive step I've taken towards
healing
And it started with something as simple as a song

I remember when you were my song
You were the lyrics that kept playing over and over again
That catchy tune engraved in my mind forever
You were the reason I received looks of annoyance
Because I couldn't get enough of you

"What is his perception of me?"
I did everything I could to be perfect
But was my passion mistaken for desperation?
I guess he saw that I didn't love myself

Oh no. The waves
They're back and more powerful than ever
forcing their way through my tear ducts and not giving tissues
the time of day to absorb every pain I feel in this moment
I don't ever want to feel like this again– but you're my favorite song

He Fears What My Eyes See In Him

My intentions were never to change you
However, I'm not doing my part as your partner
if I don't inspire you
Changing you would mean that I
never fully appreciated the greatness that you are
But your grief, your fears, your flaws, they're safe with me

You need not change your roots, my king
For you will find solace as they're planted deeply in me

Inspiration is being the best version of myself for me
while unintentionally creating an environment
that leaves you starving for your own evolution
Though once again, I still love you as you are

I draw you into my lungs, inhaling all of you
And breathe you out a little more healed and anew
But even if you never grow, my love is here to stay
I hope that I inspire you a little bit each day

Fake Quarters

His promises were like gumball jewelry
Shining with expectations to last forever
Only to expose itself as tarnished
if you keep it against your skin too long

I always thought rebuking your demons
would set your torments free
But the demon was you
And you were tarnishing me

Let It Go

Our generation has turned everything into a competition
Even love
So we stick it out with the wrong soul
Competing with our ego
because we'd rather try to make it work
than realize we failed

I affirm that some failure
Is good failure

Nüde Slumber

Tonight I sleep naked in hopes that my dreams bring me closer to you
I dream of what it feels like for your fingertips
to trace the softness of my petite curves
I dream of how your lips taste as they gently caress mine

Tonight I sleep naked to feel my skin against the sheets
Crisp and cool– the perfect temperature to be held
That's how I see us–knotted in each other

Tonight I sleep naked to feed my fantasies
Like headboard concussions solely from back shots
And twisted toe curling because you hit the right spots

Tonight I sleep naked while listening to the rain
I lay here and think of all the ways to give you brain
On my knees? Upside down? Perhaps a 69?
No matter the position, I'll always sip you dry

Ode to the Flower Below

Calmness flows through the waterfall
no rush to reach the edge
Only the anticipation
that the plunge is near
Nearby grows a selfless flower
Selfless in that—it's a portal
A portal for wandering souls
needing to learn their earthly lesson
The flower was choosy with the thorns that poked her
because arousal and pain only work together with the one you want
Her petals are stretched, wilted, and torn
so that a dream can be born
The flower never married the vines
only wanting to be securely entangled in her own roots
She grew far from those who will pluck her
to satisfy their own need for possession
For she belonged to no one but the earth she shared her roots with
She opens up to the sun
Its warmth a reminder of love
And when healing is needed
her friend Moon
is nestled above

Deeper

Insecure me used to take the knife
my lover left in my back
And throw myself against the wall
to feel something deeper

But deeper only felt good
bent over, taking his many strokes

My curves aren't meant to fit the hands of any lover
They were made just for him
Like a glass slipper, he was the perfect fit
Until his ego grew, shattering the illusion
that he was made for me

Insatiable

I like to think that you save me for last
so you can savor the best bite

It Was All Yellow...

I don't beg for the truth much these days
My intuition revealing more to me than you ever would
I just sit back quietly and observe
Most days processing feelings that don't even belong to me
But that's the price I pay for seeing the magic in you

Once our bodies melted into one it became more than physical for me
Attraction still rising but it's your soul
that steals a heartbeat from me every time we're together
I tend to cling to those moments
Realizing they're far and few between

My affection unwavering
I'd give you the world without you asking

I know your attention is divided between your options
so I wait my turn and let the excitement build
hurting my own feelings because my fantasies breed false realities
of me and you in a perfect world

My heart always leads me into the arms of fleeting love
And still my soul runs after you

Unquenched

Why did you stop admiring my petals after plucking me from my
roots?
Are they not as beautiful as the first time you discovered me?
Was my need for water too much for you?
You must be so used to having your way

Do you enjoy watching life wilt
 from the foliage that is me?

It was my pheromones that attracted your nose
A sweet scent I can no longer produce
because your selfishness wanted me at my best
but you weren't ready for the aftercare

You didn't replant me in the garden of your heart
so I can keep growing more beautifully for you
Instead, you left me on your window seal
with zero intentions of preserving me
once the sun finished me off

Perpetual Softness

Why must I be responsible for changing who I am by growing a thicker skin when the world could meet me with more softness? I never deserved calloused interactions when all I wanted was understanding. I can be accommodating but not at the cost of losing myself. I am a woman who feels— and quite intensely. But that doesn't make me a weakling. I do what most people can't. Instead of transmuting the darkest parts of myself, I accept them, lovingly. I can be quite brazen with matters of the heart, letting love lead like a bulldozer.

But be careful with me–I can build and destroy.

Inoubliable.

Fall back
Let your feelings escape you
I know your ego thrives
in nonchalant spaces
But your heart remembers
that I am the alchemist
transmuting all your pain
into eternal light

I know you're not this careless
Emotions just bury themselves
the deeper they're felt
but again, your heart knows
with me you are safe

Head in the Clouds

He didn't feel my eyes undress him
Or see I was tranced under his spell
His smile- captivating like the sun making love
to fools gold in the riverbeds

With a kiss and the pass of a blunt
he got the munchies
His taste buds craving only me

I love how passionate
His tongue dips and twirls
like a Pooh getting the
last drop of honey

And as good as I am on my knees
He didn't want me there

Read Me Often

Sometimes I feel like a bookmark in the novel of you
I've accepted my role as a placeholder
knowing your favorite chapter won't be the one
filled with our memories
But you'll come back to the pages where I rest
And when you do, I hope they bring you comfort

How did you tattoo yourself in my mind so effortlessly?
And how am I assumed the fool for caring?
My love does not require a "return to sender"
Just to be a moment in your story is enough

Kaleidoscopic Trips

You inspire me Willow
Quite the Reiki Master
Healing me as I fall into the arms of open truth
I mixed you with my friend Molly
And I swear that together we met our Creator

Swaying my body while my mind runs
through galaxy-filled gardens in the sky
I saw myself perfectly raw
as stars danced through my fingers

My soul warm and fear absent
More alive than the day I became an Aries
I laid naked on the grass wishing to bare my skin
for mister moon to kiss
Consciousness rising. Guilt surrendering. Compassion blanketing

This was spiritual
On this trip–I am unbound

Not So Gentle Reminder

You need to love me at full maximum
- Note to self

Gaia Heals

How many times will I break my own heart?
I fall too easily
I've become more in love with being on the ground
because it's the only thing willing to catch me

But laying here in the arms of Mother Nature
Is where I find rest

Home Body

It's a good thing I love the rain
because I'm willing to stand in it
with you and feel each drop
We can lay in your puddles
or rage with your thunder

I'm in no rush to find shelter
because with you, I am home
My love is our umbrella
both open and closed

I can be the roof if you need protecting
Or an open window giving your wind
the space to move freely
I could even be the sturdy foundation
when your lightening spits fire to the ground

Or I can just be still.
Just be here.
Just be present.
With you.

Love Simplified

The way I process my thoughts
before indulging in you
Is proof of my healing and growth

I won't be obsessive and crazy
Or rush the natural instinct to dive
headfirst into you

For your sake
I want love to be easy this time

Convoluted

You are the book I long to read
I want to remember all your pages
and footnotes
Poetry in your eyes every time I catch you in a gaze
Like a sponge, I absorb every detail of you
Attentiveness my strong suit
And still I find myself not fully understanding you
My favorite mystery unsolved

Timepeace

I'm deteriorating
I've succumbed to the damages of a broken heart
There's no fixing it, I fear
I'll keep it broken for now
The repair kit is becoming far too expensive
for time is not on my side

The Beggar

My whole existence relies on one thing
and one thing only. Love.
So why do I continue to run into broken people
as sensitive and as fragile as I am?

Why do I continue to spread love to people unwilling to accept it?
When will someone suffocate me with love
When will someone value me?
Take me to dinner? Buy me flowers? Pray for me?

I attract broken people because I too am broken
I dwell on the what ifs
I continue to pursue a love that only exists
in the fairytale corner of my dreams
I want you to notice me

My gapped smile
The way I only like odd numbers
The smudges on my paper because I'm a lefty
The way my lips point upwards like a turtle
How I'm adventurous, but also very scary
Those are things that capture your heart
when you love someone

But you don't
And your rejection is a reflection of why I will never be good enough

...for you.

Cyclical Disappointments

I've never been given the chance
to decide the length of my relationships lifespan
I've never felt unhappiness so crippling
that it forms the words, "It's over"
after making love the night before

Each one of you took all that I was willing to give
Your confidence was shaped solely because I lost myself
I gave you pieces of me that I should've kept sacred
I promised you forever in three words, "I love you"

Men love confidence in a woman but you never built me up
I was simply a bank and something wet to sleep in
I've never had the unfortunate feeling
of rolling over and falling completely out of love
with the most beautiful soul lying next to me

The delusion is always thinking I am more
important to love than I actually am

Freefall

Most of my life's lessons were never learned
as beautifully as I've written about them
I've made heartbreak look like waves crashing over and over
after the rage of a thundering sky—all consuming, yet destructive

I want to be kept.

Somehow, I've never quite "fallen" in love
Those are all the best love stories, when it's least expected.
But no. I chose love. Each time. I didn't fall.
I've always had a knack for being intentional

I'll learn everything there is to know about you
And keep notes within the files of my heart with your name
So when you ask, "Why me?" I'll have every detail I'll need
to paint you as the most beautiful soul

Love bombing I suppose.

This time will be different... Because I'll fall.
I'll fall at the sight of you. I'll fall when I hear your voice.
I'll fall when my eyes get wrapped up in your smile
Maybe that's the lesson—reciprocity
So fall for me... unexpectedly.

Celestial

The sun doesn't judge the darkness
and challenge him to produce light
That is the kind of love I long for
I want to tell love that I'm a blackhole
Without love needing to project it's luminosity

Fear not, the parts of me unseen
Love me as I am
Through all my voids and darkness
Our galaxies await–unbound to any rules

804

Give yourself praise, just as I do
Because whatever service you did
in the world, God orchestrated our connection
I am the manifestation of your good karma

I won't lie, the stars exploded
the moment my eyes met yours
The agreement was to stay casual
but I knew feelings would catch me
You're too special

Even simplicity has its complexities

I don't want to possess you
No—you're like the wind
Free flowing with levels of
intensity and infinite direction
When you rage and spin into a force of nature
I want to be your calm—your Sunday breeze

If the choice was mine
you'd never experience another day
not knowing what love is
Because love is me

Wildflower

I am a Forget-Me-Not
blooming in a field of roses
and you accepted all that I had to offer
Which is to be wild and free
You didn't try to change the bad girl
But you complimented the good woman in me

An audacious act of love

Journal Entry: December 1, 2021

Love does not mean the same to me that it did when I was young(er) and blinded by naivety. I've learned that I am replaceable. My lovers projections were always the fast route to destruction–never allowing me to love them fully. Did they not feel worthy of such intensity? Chasing bodies instead of learning to keep me. Did they crave my soul the way I craved theirs? Did I actually crave their soul or their attention? I mean, the same way they moved on, as did I. Each breakup left me gutted, but I prevailed. I had so many reactions–screaming, crying, self-loathing. But I always found a way to get back up and heal my heart. This time was different. This last type of hurt was unfamiliarly familiar. Was I accepting of his attention and promises because I lacked receiving those things as a child? Did hearing praises make my panties wet because I didn't get the love and recognition I craved from my father? I have realized that the blame isn't solely attached to my past lovers–I've projected my own insecurities as well. I didn't love myself enough. I didn't know how to. I didn't think it was the ultimate requirement for finding freedom. I'd never tasted peace on the tip of my tongue in this way before. Life is one big transaction; how could I not believe that love is the same? Having conditions isn't unconditional love. There is an inability to love anyone without first loving myself. So, I stand in mirrors affirming my infatuation with self. I honor her. I will heal her. I love her.

The Audacity of a Healed Woman

You must think you're so much better than me
Smiling. Radiating. Loving.
Who gave you permission to be happy?
Who gave you permission to be healed?

You're supposed to be angry
Remember the ex that broke your heart?

Who gave you permission to forgive?
All the pain you felt--you're just gonna let it all go?
Is Queen Karma going to have her moment
fucking up the lives of those who broke you?

You mean to tell me you're letting go of control?
Since when did you move on
without angrily obsessing over things you can't control?
Wasn't that fun? Weren't we bonding?
I thought we loved uncomfortable comfort
How dare you call your power back

Who gave you permission?

Simplicity

Naked, lathered in Shea Butter, and tiptoeing
around my living room while smoking a blunt
doesn't seem like a bad pastime
I was made for days like this

Other days I'm swaying my hips to Bob Marley's
"Is it love"
While making my man some breakfast
In his oversized t-shirt

I am my free-est when I'm creative
Finding excitement in cutting
Heart shaped strawberries to compliment a dish
This is the beauty of living in the moment

Unsatisfied Reflections

Trapped in a maze
Yet, devoid of amazement
Strangers treading cautiously
For change feels too drastic

Are you still my lover, oblivious to who I am?
Your arousal persists at the touch of my lips
But is it your body's response to repetition?

Lacking attention to detail
Do you even notice my body refusing your touch?

No longer my sanctuary
But a mirror reflecting our darkest facets
Despite my efforts to salvage us
You'd rather let the dust settle

Failed

"How could you move on so fast?!"
That was the question.
But my responsibility to the truth
proved you weren't ready for my answer

How could I move on so quickly?
I evolved well beyond your broken promises
You can't fool me anymore with fairytales
 of a future that doesn't exist
You were quite the actor, making me believe
 you wanted my hand in marriage
And when the director said "cut", you did just that

You didn't listen. You didn't pay attention.
Your fear of confrontation made it difficult for me to feel safe
If you can't protect me from your family
how the fuck can I believe you'd protect me from a stranger?
You let them spill all their opinions of me
And not once corrected their tongues

I filled roles that weren't mine to fill
Because I loved you
So forgive me for choosing myself this time

Jñāna

I passed out cups of accountability for everyone else to drink from and had none left for myself. It's funny, because I always prided myself on accountability and how I make people feel. I became a little slower to answer without first processing my thoughts and how they ought to be delivered to make them a little more digestible. Very little did I extend that same intentionality to myself. I was so fixated on decorating words and sentences, you know, making them prettier to understand and tastier to ingest. I needed to let people know they hurt me but I didn't want to offend their pride. I over explained way too often, as if people didn't know they were in the wrong. It was just easier to once again assume I was the problem. I fell in love with being uncomfortable and didn't notice its toxic hold until the trauma took form in the physical. Women, we carry our emotions in our hips, or so I've heard. It soon became believable as my emotions began presenting themselves outside of teary eyes. Have you tried riding the waves of your lover just to have your hips lock you away from euphoria? Those were the nights that took longer for me to peak. I had to navigate my body in new ways—a readjustment to the unhealed parts of me that were screaming for attention, and while yoga taught me patience, I still had a lot to learn about letting go. Self-realization is always the first step, and that, I've mastered.

Sweet Something

You are but a chapter in my book
Where passion and fun intertwine
Attracted to our similarities
But knowing it never goes further than this

Gemini

I can't make this poetic. No. You deserve a journal entry. It was easier to not trust you than to believe I was worthy of staying faithful to. So your role was the villain, up until you weren't. At least that's what I thought. Your bond with manipulation was more substantial than steel. I stayed so long because you were "a good guy." You worked, paid the bills, and validated me when I needed it, and somehow, that was enough. Only...it wasn't. You were calm and never reactive, forcing me to check myself often. I thought I was crazy. My traumas screamed, not getting the chance to see you rise and match my flames. In translation, you didn't care. But again, I looked at myself in the mirror and questioned why I needed a rise out of you. I watched my mom and stepdad have yelling matches and make-up afterward. That was my normal. If it's love, you'd prove it with your rage. You triggered me. I thought I was the problem for so long until lies were revealed. I later learned that you had a gambling problem. You kept me away from your family, and I figured out why at the end of it all. All the overthinking and thoughts of being crazy rushed over me. I had been gaslighted for four years. You were my first relationship after three years of abstinence. All that time, I thought I was healing to be a better partner for my next lover, who happened to be you. Instead, I was met with resistance and narcissistic tendencies. I tried to heal you. You came with traumas of your own, but the effort to overcome them was nonexistent. That's because you didn't believe you needed healing. Things just happen, and we move on. But don't you grow tired of ignoring your pain? I did. It showed up all too often in our relationship, and I wasn't comfortable settling for an empty forever. It wasn't all bad. You were the Carter to my Lee–our favorite reference. We planned dreamy futures, but you sang a different tune once your divorce was finalized. I guess we couldn't stand the rain, another favorite reference of ours; we would be so tickled harmonizing that song. I found myself reading old messages of your promises to always love me, but those were sweet lies turned bitter. "We don't have to be strangers. I want to be your friend." I think that was the message that brought the waterworks. You were my first real taste of commitment. We merged our traumas, and they intensified. We failed. You failed. I held on as long as I could and lost myself. I found myself missing parts of you...parts of us. I wasn't easy to love, but it was mutual. The sweetest Rose was the best thing that came from loving you, and to watch her grow into an array of petals is the only thing I'll miss.

The Cheat Code to Healing

< expecting pain
> accepting love

Imploded Lungs

I'm doing you a disservice
though it could be mutual
I'm not allowed to love you in
all the intensities you deserve
and what a tragedy
Because God never mentioned
love needing permission to live

Completely infatuated with you
I inhale all that you are
I drown in the sea of our memories
My only reason for saving myself
is the anticipation to make more with you

But being underwater for so long made me hopeless
And so the waves folded me in like a hug
But they didn't bring me peace
the way yours do

Just Friends

Is my absence felt?
That's been the question
as of recent
The silence, excruciatingly loud

I laid it all at your feet
My whole heart
I've never been so sure
that someone was made for me
and yet—I was so wrong

The weight of sadness
crushes my chest
as the truth is unveiled
that I was nothing more
than a distraction

...until you were ready to love her again

Attn.

From the moment I received you
I was addicted
My mind races as my pupils dilate
like a baby tasting sugar for the first time
A molecule away from being destruction
Yet, you've always tasted so sweet

You make the hairs on my body erect
I've looked for you in every person I've met
I beg for you
I accept whatever I can get from you
Because I love you

I melt every time you speak to me
Your sweet whispers send messages to self-conscious ears
Reassurance is what I need
though you only give it when you can be the master
I guess you're my ventriloquist, controlling all my existence

Unnatural—that's what you call a lack of flow
And the closer to you I get, the less I know
Or...the less I knew
Maybe it's because all of my strings are attached to you
And everything you are is everything I need
But with these scissors named "rejection"—I'm forced to be freed

Intimate Reverie

My pussy gets butterflies when I think of you
Remembering the feel of your kisses tracing my back
While you force a deeper arch, lil booty tooted up
Boy, you know my face too pretty to be in these sheets

I love demanding eye contact while I ride you until you bust
My titties cheering for you, the only encouragement you need
Nipples hard–just waiting for their moment with your warm tongue

How'd I get so lucky?
Are you the devil in disguise?
Navigating my body like you've known me in every lifetime
You're sick.

In all fairness, I may be sicker
Nasty for sure
The way my mouth handles your pretty brown curve is ungodly
I could suck and slurp and spit all day, daddy you taste so good

I'm a soaking mess every time your hands hug my throat
Which I think should be more often
Don't be gentle, I love a firm choke
You know that puts me in my place every time
Add a side of deep rough strokes
Look at you–securing your spot as the GOAT

Constellations

Falling doesn't hurt so bad anymore
I've slipped through the fingers of many lovers
The melodic moans my mouth created for them
Never tightened their grip on catching me
So I set out to be a one hit wonder

My pride evicting opportunities of being used
But it's always the soul yearning for more
I want you to experience me
Physically is too easy

Are you willing to step outside the realm of you
To fall into the light of me?
When you look into my eyes, are they the stars you wish upon?
Do I feel like love when our energies intertwine?

Creative Unions

I had the honor of orchestrating the most
intimate of unions: Pen and Paper
The way Pen caresses the smoothness of Paper
and the delicate, crisp texture that paper offers
allowing Pen to glide so eloquently
I take credit for this union
Well, perhaps not me, but rather my emotions
You see, at times, I have no one to confide in
so when people won't lend an ear
Pen and Paper are right there ready to
unite and make love out of my emotions

Soft strokes yield poems of love and joy
While pain, depression, and hurt
create a more forceful stroke forming
indentations that I dare not mention
because honestly; who really talks about pain?

Pen and Paper make the most passionate love
when depression strikes
Those feelings, vast and chaotic
nearly drove Pen and Paper to divorce
Which was all my doing of course
Because I stopped having emotions
I stopped caring and dreaming
I tried hiding my pain and ended up feigning
I needed to nurture more love, even if not for me

So Pen and Paper made a baby
They named her "Fresh Start"

And she blossomed with words
Her touch was gentle, her inspiration profound
She was created from the ecstasy of a love unbound

Red String of Fate

How many times have I passed the soul
wishing upon the same star as me?
Two hopeless romantics
building walls that put Chinas to shame
Begging the universe for connection
when all it takes is the removing of the first stone
I'll take the chisel to my heart & open space for you, my flame

My love has no limits, truly unconditional
Is that why we've not met?
Are you not ready to be swallowed by the wave of me?
Encompassing all that God is with my sweet words
and knowing every ounce that is you

How is that for energy?
Follow the cord that connects us in every lifetime
Until we find each other in this one

Oceanic Dreams

I wonder how the ocean feels knowing that I'm much deeper
Instead of waves your touch causes trembling quakes
I whisper sweet thoughts into an ear full of wonders
I soft suck your lips–Imagination is all you can suffice
Once feeling the wet plumpness of my soft lips
not of my mouth but right below my hips
Your shaft grows to great lengths
Excited to be the anchor in an ocean so free
Your mouth waters causing you to go down
Face first into the realm of a spring
I feel the strength of your arms pick me up
And place me on the ocean floor
Knees grounded and mouth open
I suck the tip of what seems like heaven
I hear you moan as you deep stroke my throat
If this is what drowning feels like
Then I won't fight it
After swallowing every drop of your imagination
I float on your surface, riding your mind to a place of bliss
I softly caress the pounding in your chest that creates
subliminal beats of confusion
Following the movements of the waves
We make our way out of orgasmic fantasies
For only a moment, we shared oceanic dreams

The Only Exception

You were right, you know?
I don't know who you are in a relationship
But I like to believe that a woman like me is
worth the best version of you—because I am
Even with my boundaries enforced
your energy still lingers, like my favorite scent
which funnily enough, was always *you*

Heaven is Waiting

I'm ready for my flowers
but plant them next to me
and water them with your tears
while you grieve who I once was

Speak the kindest of words
and share your favorite memories of us
My soul is much too kind for earth
I belong amongst the angels

The love I crave is godly
I didn't want to break your heart
though this pain I carry, hurts far more
In God's arms, I'll finally find rest

I'm ready for my flowers
and the look in God's eyes
when he tells me "good job"
Even knowing I could've been better

I won't be anyone's favorite
until I'm gone and all that's left
are memories of me
Why was it so hard for me to be chosen?

I'm ready for my flowers
I have a date with God

Trauma Bound

You're so in love with the comfort of emptiness and chaos that you're not willing to give peace and unconditional love a try. How does it feel to spend years with the one you love just to beg for the bare minimum and then meet someone who gives it so effortlessly, without you ever having to ask. You don't think you deserve reciprocity, even though that's all you want. So, instead of being in a union that's fulfilling, you marry your traumas. Merging more pain and bonding to an idea of an unrealistic forever. But your eternity is supposed to be restful. It's supposed to feel like laying on the chest of your favorite person and finding gratitude in the moment of listening to the calming rhythm of their heartbeat. Love isn't chaos. Love isn't possessive. Love is *me*.

Pointofyou.

When you say I'm emotional
is that a reflection of your insecurities?
My passion can be intimidating
For I am a child born of fire
but so are you, Leo
And somehow, I assumed you'd survive my heat

Admittedly, I'm not to be tamed
And I'll submit, but not to the inner child of you
I know the expectation isn't to fall for me
So my hopes don't get as high as me and you
tangled up together with a blunt in rotation

How is it that my energy attracts souls with your M.O.?
Is it the love I exude? My confidence?
Or is it the passionate rage between my thighs?
You said, "This is daddy's pussy"
So forgive me for thinking it only belonged to you

Those words were never said again
It's easy to assume you didn't
want to get caught up
But either way—she's still *yours*
Always choosing you
Is fucking me the only time you've felt how
deep you can go?
Our eyes caught up in the moment
not realizing that with each stroke
I'm healing you

You won't experience love
Until you experience me

Return to Sender

You're proof of God's love
I know he favors me most
because you were unexpected
and he let me borrow you
for a season

I prayed for more
selfishly hoping to
be the one occupying
your heart
But love doesn't work
that way

God's plans for you are
much greater than mine
So selflessly and lovingly
I release you

Because love isn't possessive
And he knows your heart
far better than I

Disillusioned

I was gonna text you today
But fear trickled to the tips of
my fingers and brought them to a halt
I started to spell out *"I love you"*
Yet saved myself the embarrassment

I've been known to wear a
clown mask at times—heart fully exposed
Falling more in love with hope
than accepting my reality

She's lucky.
Getting chance after chance with you
when all I need is *one*
I'd give you infinities
but I already give so much
knowing your heart is elsewhere

You confide in me
You deep dive in me
A healthy obsession
I can be that for you

I want to praise you
Because I crave you
A delicacy
Made only for my tongue

Fire & Desire

I thought I could do it
You know, love you a little less
But you don't deserve a skinny love
I wanted you to have all of me

You played a dangerous game
Starting a fire in my soul
that burns only for you
And yet, you extinguish it

I keep setting myself ablaze
As you throw water on me
Who are you trying to save?
Me or you?

Your rejection is a hard acceptance
Knowing we used to be tangled up in each other
I didn't fall under the gaze of delusion
No—I know the feelings were mutual

There's no greater passion than patience
Because even when the fire consumes me
The burns prove my loyalty to wait for you

The smoke smothers my lungs
But you've always had a way of taking my breath away
My handsome Leo
Why do our fires clash
when they should be merged as one?

Newfound Love

Take the most precious materials of the earth
And multiply that by me
A rarity, indeed
That's what I am

I've never been scared of snakes
As I was always shedding my skin
Shedding pieces of me
to better camouflage myself
and fit the criteria of the world

All I wanted was love
God's love is all-consuming
And yet, I never felt it
until I went inward

A Phoenix
That's the kind of power I hold
Transforming from dust
into a rage of confidence
My light enough to brighten
the depths of the devils soul

The lessons learned
almost sucked the life out of me
But I prevailed
I should've been gone long ago
Oh.. but purpose

My energy like a magnet
My love like the sweetest dessert
My soul like the warmth of the sun
kissing you on your forehead

I was always the magic

Fading

What happens when I stop writing about you?
When my pen trembles with dry tears across the
surface of paper untouched because I've exhausted
my sweet words of affirmations to you?

The Sun and Her Clouds

It's funny how I've always assumed that choosing you was the same as choosing me. Because when I choose to love you... all of you, it brings me a joy so unexplainable that it feels like I'm loving myself. I'm spoiling myself. I'm making me happy because loving you sends fire through every cell in my veins. But maybe it was the idea of you that I created in my mind to escape reality. Maybe it was my imagination that made the truth an easier pill to swallow. You were only special because of me. I was enchanted by my own magic to see you as everything perfect. My inner child adored you. That's who kept choosing you. A little girl fearful of abandonment and riddled with self-limiting beliefs that she'll never be good enough. But for you, I was. You complimented me often and helped me rediscover myself. Rediscover my confidence. You made me feel loved—how low must the bar be for you to have done so little and make me feel so much? When we were skin to skin and caught up in each other's eyes is when I felt the safest. But maybe that never happened. Maybe we never experienced passion and it's been one sided this whole time. Perhaps placing you on a pedestal that reached the gates of Heaven is where my delusions turned clinical. You're not the only one who thinks I'm crazy. I'm convinced, myself, that all the strings aren't attached. I've never experienced this version of me either... so we're both confused. And yet, you get to walk away while I'm stuck learning why I feel like it's okay to minimize myself to fit into your world. Radiant is my soul—enough light to compete with the sun. So how can I share my light with the whole world, when it's always blanketing *you?*

Bibliosexual

I'm the perfect novel
If you want to explore my mind
Let's bookmark the frontal lobe for now
The discoveries you find in other rooms
Will help you better understand the traumas
That rest there

Let me be the book that you read
And dare not judge my cover
As it's hard, and I may seem tough
But my words breed both love and softness

Hot off the press is where
Our bodies can intertwine
Spread open my thighs
And lick the pages
While the ink is still wet

Maybe blur the lines a bit

The Prize

I laugh at desperation.
Because who am I but royalty
Demanding of the highest praise?

Thought Shift

I realized the cups of accountability I was passing out to everyone else was necessary. I wasn't in the wrong for forcing people to see the negative impacts of their actions. Yes, my reaction to the hurt and disrespect required therapy, but the realization set in that I was allowing people to mistreat me because I viewed everything as a projection. I was too understanding. Fuck that.

Thirty.

You know what you're doing, binding my love for you
with moments that feel like dreamy flashbacks in the movies
with 80's music playing in the background
Those were always the best love scenes

The song was fitting
Little Red Corvette blasting through the speakers
Hennessey on our breath as we drove up I-20
I cry at how beautiful that moment felt

Your wild side is the flame and I'm the moth
Forgive my "scaredy cat" anxieties
I just can't imagine life without you
So it's my job to keep you safe

We laugh at me being a sleepyhead
But in my dreams is where everything is perfect with you
It's where I get to hear your I love you's
And you don't hold back your passion

I get high off you without ever touching the blunt
It is with you that I am my freest
I'd worship every ounce of you if you'd let me

I didn't lie, you know?
My pussy is still yours for the keeping
I only hope you weren't babbling
When you said that dick is mine
You know I don't like sharing when it comes to you

I wish you could see yourself through my eyes
But that's still not enough
I'm the best option for you, I promise
I've always had your best interest at heart

Prince said it best
You need to find a love that's gonna last

Green Lights

I don't think I am a woman to be kept, though I am not entirely sure. Of course I'm the prize, but I won't sit on the shelf of you, collecting dust and inconsistent adoration. I tend to outgrow my lovers. I am not willing to compromise my growth and evolution for stagnancy and lack of motivation. I love the thrill of life. The unexpected. I require my lovers to study me with avidity—to know me, you must crave my entire being. All or nothing. You must feel me beyond the wetness that swallows you whole. I'm deeper than what lies between the thickness of my thighs. My mind is like an intricately designed web. I like to believe that with each forehead kiss, I am feeding you wisdom. When you share your dreams with me, they become seeds that I plant in my womb and nurture until God brings them to life. My tongue dances behind clenched teeth, awaiting the taste of you. On bended knees is when my throat is in tune to sing your praises and affirmation. It's funny; I stumble into the arms of men who want all of me and none of me, simultaneously. I paved roads of availability, with not a stop sign in sight—zero boundaries. Just green lights that seemed to only work at night.

l'étoile

I could get lost in you, easily.
Free-falling into the multi-hyphenate
that you are wouldn't be a fear of mine
even if you decided not to catch me
Because what is a safe space if it isn't you?

Even your absence is comforting
Because your energy still lingers
I've not been shot by Cupid's bow
No. My love is far more intentional
I do, however, hold a heightened admiration
But I dare not divulge
the glass home that is my heart
As time will unequivocally reveal all

I have to meet you with caution
For you are so beautifully complex
That I'm forced to adjust my crown
before introducing our royalties

Our minds non-congruent
And yet, we still leave space to
Innerstand that our differences
are mere conformities
with different lenses
How is that for an oxymoron?

Your layers have layers, tenfold
And until God decides we've
done our parts in each other's lives
I'll continue exploring the

fun house that is your mind
Visiting all the rooms
even the ones filled with monsters
But only if you trust me with the keys

Beloved

You sweet, precious girl
Please wipe your tears
Place your worries in my hands
And find the peace you never experienced

You deserved to keep your spark
And not dimmed by the insecure
All the dreams you have right now
Can easily be yours

You deserved to keep those dreams alive
And dance in all your fantasies
For you were only a little girl
Escaping toxic realities

You are worthy of infinite love
Just as you are
Proving yourself all these years
Did not get you far

Putting others before yourself
Beautiful is your soul
But it's time to rest your insecurities
As healing is the goal

Final Note

Again, ten years. It took me ten years to finally put myself first. To finally accept the truth for what it is, and that is this: I am loveable. I am always chosen. I am worthy. I wasn't always the problem, though I know that the boundaries I lacked created a lot of hurt. How could I be upset with anyone else but myself? My boundaries didn't just lack in my romantic relationships, but platonic and familial as well. I fell into a lot of toxic patterns. I learned that self-realization is the first step. How do I take what I learned and apply it? There is only so much healing that one can experience. I won't ever be completely free from the flaws of pain. And that's okay. I spend more time in gratitude. I keep my mind clear. I don't have expectations anymore. It's funny how I thought all my lovers were made just for me—a recurring theme. I mean, I guess they were. Each the same lesson with a different face. I wanted unwavering commitment, but they were just reflecting what I was putting out. How could they commit to me, or find value in the goddess that I am, if I never actually believed I was a goddess? It was attention I was seeking...validation. Not love. I never needed any of them to crown me worthy. My confidence now, unshakeable. No longer the beggar, but the chooser, and my, how choosy I've become. I healed wounds for generations to come, and I am only getting started. I am proud of the woman I am. My inner child bursting with joy as I now know how to love her correctly. I've given my entire being to everyone else. Now my devotion belongs to me.

Meet the Author

Hey there, I'm Trenessa. I was born and raised about 30 miles west of Atlanta, Georgia, in a city named Douglasville. As the oldest of six children, I found my passion for writing at an early age when I began journaling about my day. I fell in love with poetry, penning heartfelt poems together for family members. Overtime, writing became my best friend and only means of self-expression, giving me the space to embrace my vulnerability while validating each passing emotion.

Beyond writing, I have practiced cosmetology off and on over the last 11 years, earning my licensure one year after graduating high school. I enjoy combining my love for art with my love for making people look and feel beautiful about themselves. Some of my hobbies include meditating, yoga, absorbing nature, and spending time with those close to me. I am a dog and cat mom to my fur babies, Arielle and Santana. A growing passion of mine is sharing my love through cooking. Food has always been a way to bring people together and merge cultures, so I find it one of my favorite love languages.

In my debut, self-published book, The Evolution of Her Perception, I invite you into my world, where themes of self-love, trauma, growth, forgiveness, and self-discovery intertwine; creating the safe space you need to humanize your own feelings and heal beyond the surface.